MW01172968

Scripture references are from the King James Version of the Bible unless otherwise noted.

Definitions are from the Merriam Webster Dictionary.

Copyright Information

TXu002185436

Library of Congress Control Number:

2019921252

Spiritual Stagnation

(Forever Changed)

By

Mozell L. Bryant

Words From the Author

My name is Mozell Bryant. I have always had a deep love for writing even as a child. With so many things going on in this world, we as saints must be equipped with all our weapons of warfare. I am hoping and praying that all that read this book truly will be "Forever Changed"! God inspired me to write this book. I hope you enjoy it. This is just the beginning. There will be many books to come. I have two published poems. My first book, "Wait – The Importance of You" was written to awaken and alert young people to achieve the greatness inside of them! God bless you and thank you for taking time to read and hopefully and prayerfully YOU WILL BE FOREVER CHANGED!

Love you,

 Mozell

Acknowledgment Page

I give God all the glory, honor and praise for His leading and guidance in making this book become a reality. It is because of His pouring into me that I have succeeded in accomplishing this goal. It is with heartfelt thanks and appreciation to so many people that helped make this book a reality. Special thanks and appreciation to my husband, Matthew Bryant, for his encouragement; Pastor Okoye Morgan for encouragement and support of the visions God gave me and Just to name a few supporters: Maria Bryant-Jones, Jimmie L. Smiley, Malinda Smith, Matherleen Snell, ,Bettye Anderson, Patricia Sanders and Mary Moore.

Table of Contents

Table of Contents (Cont'd)

Challenges:

INTRODUCTION
STOP SPIRITUAL STAGNATION

It is time to Stop Spiritual Stagnation! It is time to Grow Spiritually! It is time to let go of whatever has you bound! It is time to let go and let God renew your mind! It is time to be renewed and restored to Christ 24/7! It is time to be redeemed and reconciled back to God! It is time to be transformed by the renewing of your mind that you may prove the good, acceptable and perfect will of God for you (Romans 12:2).

It is time to ask God to change you for God is the only one that can change man! It is time to forget those things behind and press towards the mark of a high calling in Christ Jesus! It is time to be set free! It is time to seek God while He may be found and call upon Him while He is yet near! It is time to be stedfast and unmovable! It is time to let Jesus come in! Won't you let Him come into your heart?

What is Spiritual Stagnation? Stagnation means: To cease to flow or run. To cease to develop, advance, or change; to become idle. You are just stuck in a place and cannot move due to circumstances, people, problems and situations that are beyond your control. You are in a place where you keep going around in circles!

You are stagnated when you cease to grow. You cannot get beyond a certain point because things or people laid stumbling blocks in your path. You are stagnated! It is time to be set free! It is time to Let Go and Let God have it all! It is time to cast all your cares upon Christ for He cares for you!

 Spiritual Stagnation happens when you allow yourself to become bound by things, sin, problems, situations, people, circumstances or the past. Your spirit man seems to get weakened by disturbances that distract or confuse you; depression, discontentment or other things that seem to attack you personally. The enemy uses these things to deceive the saints. If you are not careful and prayerful, it will come upon you while you are not in tuned with God. Stay connected. Maintain a relationship with the Savior.

If you do not have your mind focused on God, things will take root in your heart! When it takes root in your heart, it is hard to be set free of its hold on you. Once in your heart then it is on your mind at times when you should be doing or thinking of something else. It keeps coming back to you as if it happened "just now". When you talk about it to someone else, you find yourself addressing the conversation to that person as if they were the ones that hurt you. You find yourself saying, you cannot say that to me! It has a hold on your heart and mind. You feel like you are talking to the person right then even though it happened a week, a month and sometimes years ago. Your heart is having a hard time of letting it go.

The Scripture says, For out of the abundance of the heart the mouth speaks (Luke 6:45). Whatever is in your heart will come out of your mouth. We must ask God to create in us a clean heart and renew a right spirit within us. You may find yourself "talking differently" about things because your heart has been hurt or broken.

Remember the Lord is close to those that are of a broken heart (Psalm 34:18a). Just trust in God with all your heart and lean not unto your own understanding, in all your ways acknowledge Him and He shall direct your path (Prov. 3:5-6). Let Him have it! Christ makes the difference!

When your heart is hurt or broken, it sometimes causes a stumbling block in your life. You are no longer in tuned to God's word because the pain in your heart will not allow you to let go of the past. The past is now dictating your present words and sometimes feelings and actions. The past is now directing your future mindset and feelings about things in your future. The past seems to not want to let go of its hold on you! It is easier to hold on and not let go because it's more comfortable and familiar to you.

Letting go requires a lot of effort and dedication on your part. It requires praying and fasting for 'this kinds' to be loosed from your heart, mind, soul and spirit. When we have 'this kinds' {Matt. 17:21) in our lives, fasting and praying breaks the hold that the past tries to hinder your natural and spiritual growth.

Spiritual Stagnation grows in you and manifests itself in you sometimes without your knowledge. Your spirit man has been so hurt or broken that you feel tired a lot and you have not done anything to be tired. You find yourself angry without a reason. It will drain your strength to hold on. It says in

Isaiah 41:10 that God will be with you, strengthen you, help you and uphold you with the right hand of His righteousness.

It is a marvelous thing just knowing that God will be with you no matter what you may go through. God promises to strengthen, help and uphold you with His right hand of righteousness. God always keep His promises. You must seek God's help. He is an ever-present help in the time of trouble. Cast all your cares upon God for He cares for you.

Spiritual Stagnation happens when you allow yourself to get caught up with the cares of this world. The cares of this world will have you so confused about even the smallest things. It will have you seeking others for help when you know the Word says, seek ye first the kingdom of God and His righteousness and all these things shall be added unto you (Matthew 6:33)! It is better to have confidence in God and not man. Man will fail you but there is no failure in God!

The cares of this world will have you bound by things that have nothing to do with you. The cares of this world will rob you of your belief. The cares of this world will dictate how you should feel and what you should think about other people. It starts with little things. Getting you to accept things as they appear instead of how they really are.

You must be sober and vigilant because the adversary, the devil, as a roaring lion, walketh about, seeking whom he may devour. If you are not sober and vigilant, you may be consumed by the cares of this world. Do not be deceived!

It is time to allow the Holy Ghost to have its way in your life! The Holy Ghost will keep you if you want to be kept! The Holy Ghost will fill you if you want to be filled! The Holy Ghost will lead you if you want to be led! The Holy Ghost will deliver you if you want to be delivered! The Holy Ghost will set you free if you want to be set free! The Holy Ghost will come unto you if you seek Him! If you want the Holy Spirit, you must ask God for it (Luke 11:13c).

The Word admonishes us to tarry until we receive power (Acts 1:8a). The Holy Ghost will give you directions if you seek Him! The Holy Spirit will give you revelations if you desire things to be revealed. The Holy Spirit will preserve you, maintain and sustain you.

You have to ask God to give you wisdom and revelation in knowing Him so that the eyes of your understanding will be enlightened so that you may know what is the hope of His calling, and what the riches of the glory of His inheritance in the saints. (Eph. 1:17a). When God gives you revelation and wisdom in knowing Him, your eyes can see beyond where you are to where He is taking you! Get to know now who God is for yourself.

The Spirit also helps our infirmities: for we know not what we should pray for as we ought: but the Spirit itself makes intercession for us with groanings which cannot be uttered (Romans 8:26). When you are going through or have physical weakness, problems, situations, ailment or lack of strength and do not know what or how to pray, the Holy Spirit prays on your behalf.

The Holy Spirit makes intercessions for the saints according to the will of God (Romans 8:27b). The Spirit takes your prayers to God!

Spiritual stagnation happens to the best of us. It comes upon us unawares. It comes upon us sometimes without our having an inclination of what is happening to us. It will steal your joy. It will steal your peace. It will steal your drive and dreams. It will steal your personal desires to want to live holy. It will steal your happiness. It will steal your ability to be you. It will steal your determination. It will steal your mind. It will steal your dedication right in front of you. You may not be able to make clear decisions not only spiritual but natural as well. It will rob you of your ability to think objectively about things that otherwise would have not been a problem. It will steal your drive to even pray like you used to. It will drain your strength out of you! It will make you tired of performing simple tasks. It will have you making bad decisions based upon how you feel at the moment. It will have you saying and doing things that are not of you.

Spiritual Stagnation will have you withdrawing from people that have been your friend for years. It will make you want to just be alone. Spiritual Stagnation will drain your laughter right out your mouth. You must stand firm in your unwavering faith and belief, determination and adherence; firmly secured (stedfast and unmovable) to the word of the Lord (1 Cor. 15:58a).

Idle hands are the devil's workshop and idle lips are his mouthpiece (Prov. 4:27). Idling is dangerous to your spiritual and natural man. When we have nothing to do or do not keep our mind stayed on Jesus, our mind turns to evil thoughts and from thoughts to words and maybe wrong actions. Jesus promised us perfect peace if we keep our minds focused on Him. If you fill your heart and mind with songs of praise, prayers and the Word, you will be strengthened and sustained by God.

Spiritual Stagnation is very deadly. It leaves you with a feeling of emptiness. It will rob you of your desire to live a holy life because you can become so consumed with the cares of this life. This is all temporary. Do not allow people, problems, things or situations to make you lose your pathway to Glory! Be stedfast and unmovable! God specializes in loving us, helping us and keeping us from danger seen and unseen.

Always forgive everyone in your past that hurt you, harm you, talked about you, put you down, lied on you, deceived you, didn't treat you the way you thought you should have been treated, handled you wrong, used you, persecuted you or scandalized your name! It does not matter what was said, let it go! It may have really embarrassed you, let it go! They may have put you down in front of others, let it go! Let Go and Let God deliver you from you!

Most importantly, you must forgive yourself! Forgive yourself for bad decisions, mistakes you made, whether real or imagined! Let God deliver you from you! Forgive yourself for not having the wisdom to make different choices in your life. Forgive yourself for allowing others to tell you what to think and do. Forgive yourself so that you can grow beyond and past anything that has you bound or stagnated.

Let Go and Let God deliver you from the past that keeps showing up in your future! The past sometimes makes such a drastic change in how you feel and see things in the present. Better is the end of a thing than its beginning (Ecclesiastes 7:8). God instructs us to come unto Him all that are heavy burdened, and He will give us rest (Matthew 11:28)!

God is waiting at the door of your heart for you to let Him in! He is standing at the door of your heart knocking. He said if you hear His voice and open the door, He will come into you and sup with you (Revelation 3:20). Won't you let Him in! Let Him in to set you free from whatever has you bound.

The past belongs to God anyways! Stop hanging on to past thoughts that affect your actions, thinking and loving today! The stress of the past will depress you TODAY! Let Go and Let God set you free to conquer and fulfill your purpose! Let Go Today!

Let us remember the Word of God speaking to our hearts that says, He that saith he is in the light, and hateth his brother, is in darkness even until now. He that loveth his brother abideth in the light, and there is none occasion of stumbling in him. But he that hateth his brother is in darkness, and walketh in darkness, and knoweth not *whither* he goeth, because that darkness hath blinded his eyes (1 John 2:9-11).

It is time to Stop Spiritual Stagnation. It is time to stop hating your brother or sister. It is time to walk in the light! It is time to take the blinders off so you can fully see what's in front of you! It is time to stop stumbling! It has time to come out of the darkness that binds you to a past that no longer exists but is still coming back to mind to keep you bound. Let Go and Let God deliver you! It is time to walk in the light and have no occasion for stumbling! You can stand on God's word. God won't fail you!

It is time to come out of darkness. It is time to let go of hate because it stagnates your growth. You can never grow completely when you are bound by the Spirit of Hate. Hate will devour everything you stand for because you are trapped in the darkness of your mind and you cannot truly see which way to go. Let it go. God gave us commandments to love one another. What's love got to do with it? If you do not love others, God can't dwell in you. You must love, not because of, but despite how you are treated. It is about your soul salvation. It is about your spiritual growth. You can't and won't see Jesus with hate in your heart. Let go and let God's light shine in you. Again, the Word is speaking to you about the importance of loving one another. You cannot even expect to live with Jesus with hate in your heart. God is love and we must love one another.

The Word of God instructs us that if the world hate you, we know that we have passed from death unto life, because we love those that hate us. If you do not love your brother, you abide in death. Also, whosoever hates his brother is a murderer: and no murderer hath eternal life abiding in him (1 John 3:13-15).

Beloved, let us love one another: for love is of God; and every one that loveth is born of God, and knoweth God. He that loveth not knoweth not God; for God is love (1 John 4:7-8). If you do not love others, you don't know God.

CHALLENGE
Holding On

If only the pure in heart shall see God (Matthew 5:8), how do you even expect to go to heaven when you are still holding onto things done to you in your heart; things said about you; how you were handled wrong; or what your mom or dad did or did not do? You will be going through life with a shadow of the past just hanging around in your mind showing itself at inopportune moments in your present. Past hurtful thoughts bring about present frustrations!

Undealt with issues, no apology from your abuser; or you just can't let it go; lies told on you and deliberate deceptions that happened in your past that are now showing up in your present day to rob you of your future goals, plans and purpose. Do not hold yourself back from your own blessings.

You must stay connected to Christ Jesus. Stay in your Word. Pray without ceasing. Your peace, your fullness of joy and happiness is yours. Recover and Reclaim it all in the name of Jesus!

I know it is hard to believe but it's not flesh and blood. It looked like flesh and blood when it was directed to you. The enemy sowed things into you while you were young or unlearned and has come back later to harvest what he sowed. The devil is a liar. Satan the Lord rebuke you!

No weapon formed against you shall prosper. God is bigger than anything the enemy forms against you. Our God can deliver you from your past hurts and brokenness. No battle can defeat you because the battle is not yours, it is the Lord's!

There is danger in holding on! There is no hurt like Church hurt! Church hurt is bad because when you go to church, you never expect to be hurt by your sister or brother in Christ in church because it is the House of God! It hurts so bad! The words were so mean and hurtful! Let it go! They lied on you! Let it go!

There are church goers that are going to hell. There are many that teach, preach, pray and dance in church that are going to hell because it is a form of godliness denying the power of God. Be holy! Be righteous! Be holy, for our God is holy, and holiness without which no man shall see the Lord! Treat others the way you want to be treated even if they do not treat you right. Live, walk and talk so that God is pleased with you! Love those that treat you wrong or hate you! Let it go!

Don't get weary in well doing! Let it go! Keep on being who God says you are despite what others say or do! Treat them right even if they treat you wrong! Let it go! Love is the key! Love those that talk about you or say hurtful words to you! Let it go!

There's danger is holding onto past hurts. If you do not let it go, you will become enslaved by the things people do to you! Let it go! Let go and let God deliver you from you! Let God have it!

Let Go and Let God have your cares! You must stay prayed up. Just remember that you are not alone for God said He would never leave you nor forsake you. God is always beholding the righteous and His ears are always open to your cry. The eyes of the Lord are upon them that fear Him, upon them that hope in His mercy (Psalm 33:18).

Let go and let God fill you up with supernatural agape love and joy unspeakable. Be who God called you to be. Be all He called you to be.

Let God bless you with all He promised to you in His Word. The Word says that if you hearken diligently unto the voice of the Lord thy God, to observe and to do all His commandments which He commands this day that the Lord will set you on high above all the nations of the earth and all these blessings shall come on you and overtake you if you hearken unto the voice of the Lord thy God. You would be blessed in the city and blessed in the field; blessed when you come in and go out (Deuteronomy 28:1-3, 6).

Won't you let Him bless you and open unto you His good treasure, bless all the work of your hands, and you will lend and not borrow (Deuteronomy 28:12). Position yourself to receive God's provisions. Let Go and Let God heal, deliver, set you free and bless you!

The Holy Spirit can heal all your past hurts and renew, revive, restore, redeem and reconcile you back to God. Just acknowledge God in all your ways, trust also in Him with all your heart and He shall direct your paths (Proverbs 3:5).

So, Love your enemies. Show Godly love to all. Delight yourself in the Lord and He shall give you the desires of your heart (Psalm 37:4). Make sure all your ways and actions are directed to the glory of God. Do what God expects you to do. Love and kindness are the key even when the other person does not show it or deserve it.

It is about kingdom work. It is about your soul salvation and your heart, for only the pure in heart shall see God. It is about being a vessel set aside for the Master's use. God cannot use you fully if the enemy still has a hold on you from the past.

The past belongs to the Lord. Let God have it! Be free! Free your heart, mind, soul and spirit to be all you were anointed, appointed, destined and ordained to be! Everyone cannot do this because they are not all on meat but still on milk (Hebrews 5:13-14). Everyone is not well versed in the Word of God.

You will need to fast and pray to be victorious to overcome obstacles. Obstacles are meant to be overcome. Our God is bigger than any obstacles, problems, situations, sickness or circumstances you may encounter.

You will need to take a walk with God through the Word. You will need to fast and pray to be victorious and overcome obstacles, problems, circumstances, sickness, illnesses or the past. Our God is bigger than anything that you may encounter. If God brings you to it, He will bring you through all of it. All things will work together for your good because you are the called according to His purpose.

You have to study to show yourself approved (2 Timothy 2:15). Ask God to let the Word take root in your heart. The Word of God is so powerful. When everything else has failed, the Word will stand. Heaven and earth may pass away, but the Word of God will stand! Stand on the Word of God. Look to the author and finisher of your faith for your deliverance and victory in all things. You are more than a conqueror through Christ Jesus.

Let us love one another for love is of God and everyone that loves is born of God and knows God. If you do not love, you don't know God for God is love. (I John 4:8). We know that we dwell in Him and He dwells in us, because He hath given us of His Spirit. As God is, so we must be in our daily walk. Let us have the mind of Christ. God has a greater good and greater purpose just for you! Let us work towards having a pure heart with meekness, for the meek shall inherit the earth!

No Relationship with God! No Power! No Connection! You must have a connection with God as with an iron that needs power to heat up and work so does our spirit need to be connected for power! No connection! No power!

You can buy a $200 iron but, if you do not plug it in for connection, it won't get any power. We need power from God but must connect to him to access His power.

We need power to walk right, talk right, live right, do right, treat one another right, be compassionate to one another.

We do not have to fear when we are connected to God's power for God hath not given us the spirit of fear, but of power, and of love, and of a sound mind.

When we are connected, we shall receive power, after that the Holy Ghost is come upon us. For the kingdom of God is not in word, but in power. No connection! No power!

Connection to God gives us power to tread on serpents and scorpions, and over all the power of the enemy: and nothing shall by any means hurt us. No connection! No power!

We can access the power of God through prayer, fasting, praising and reading His word. Through this, we can get to know what the exceeding greatness of His power to us-ward is who believe, according to the working of His mighty power. More connection! More Power! Stay Connected! Stay Strong! Stay plugged into Jesus! He is always on the mainline. You can call Him up and tell Him what you want!

The Same Holy Spirit that impregnated Mary the Mother of Jesus has the Same Power Today to impregnate with the Same Power to deliver you and bring you through every situation, sickness, illness, disease, problem or circumstance and deliver you out of all your trials, tribulations or circumstances that you may encounter and make you victorious with the Same Power!!

Just hold onto God's unchanging hand and let go of anything that binds you or stagnates your spiritual growth!

CHALLENGE
Ambassadors For Christ

As Ambassadors of Christ, we must be righteous so that our effectual, fervent prayers will avail much for problems, strongholds, situations, circumstances, diseases, illnesses, sicknesses and family.

As Ambassadors of Christ, we must humble ourselves and pray, seek God, and, turn from our wicked ways so that we can hear from heaven and God will forgive our sins and heal our land (2 Chronicles 7:14)!

As Ambassadors of Christ, we must teach others to seek first the kingdom of God and His righteousness and ALL the things that they need will be added (Matthew 6:33).

As Ambassadors of Christ, we must study to show ourselves approved so that we can rightly divide the Word and not be ashamed. God sent His Word to heal but if we are only hearers and not doers of the Word, we deceive our own selves (James 1:22). If you are a hearer of the word of God and not a doer, you are like a person looking at your face in a glass and go your way and forget what manner/kind of person you were (James 1:23-24).

As Ambassadors of Christ, we know that we are in a war and the battle is not ours but the Lord's. He will fight for us (Exodus 14:14). We are more than conquerors and the weapons of our warfare are mighty through the pulling down of strongholds. Also, we know that it is not flesh and blood, but spiritual wickedness in high places! We got to stand for holiness and righteousness! It is time to Rise Up and Stand Up for Righteousness!

What if the reason you are experiencing lack in our life; sickness or diseases; getting weary in well doing; finding it hard to press towards the mark for a high calling in Christ Jesus; hard to let go of the past hurts and pains; getting caught up with the cares of this world; anger causing you to sin; not so easy to forgive and let it go; is because your fire has gone out. Maybe you lost your zeal and passion for Christ because you had a flicker and did not realize it. You just may need the Fire of the Holy Spirit to be rekindled or reignited within you.

As Ambassadors, we must be meet for the Master's use and a vessel of honor. We must stay prayed up and fasting to access the power that God has given to us. God allows us to go through some things to wake us up. As Ambassadors, we must be careful of nothing! God will come through for us every time!

We must spend time studying His Word and fall more in love with Jesus. We must work on our personal relationship with Christ or our fire will die. We need more power! Spend some quality time with the Lord and tarry to receive the power you need.

Considering God's imminent return, you must live lives that would please Him every day until He returns. Keep the fire going, and, if need be, rekindle the fire of your passion and love for Christ through constant love for one another, prayer and fasting.

Lord, Rekindle the fire in my life and let it burn off anything that is not like You in Jesus name! Lord, help us to be the best Ambassador for You.

As Ambassadors of Christ, we have a charge to keep. We must diligently carry out our missions and assignments so that God will get the glory out of it. We must be that light that sits on a hill so that others are drawn to the light. Jesus is the light that will shine in and through your life. Your light should be reflective of who you serve. The light should always shine even in the midst of controversy. Let your light shine through obstacles, gossip, problems, put downs, lies, disappointments, trials and tribulations. Let your light shine so others can find their way to Christ. Let the light of Christ show up in your walk and in your talk. Be an example of a True Ambassador!

CHALLENGE
Hatred In A Nation

When a Nation allows hatred to run rampant, it is doomed! Hatred is like cancer. It starts at one part and sometimes for no apparent reason it flows to unaffected parts and keeps going, unless caught in time!

When you allow hatred to live in you, it will not only extend to the persons you do not like, but it will flow over to your loved ones because it has no barriers. When you let the dog out, he will attack whatever gets in his way whether real or imagined.

Hatred proves to be the culprit in the world by which one person destroys another person for reasons real or imagined. Its ugliness may extend in any direction. Hatred stirs up strife, but love coves all sins (Proverbs 10:12). The Word of God tells us that if a man says he loves God and hates his brother, he is a liar (I John 4:20). We must love one another. It is a commandment. Love even your enemies!

Don't get it twisted: Prayer changes things! The weapons of our warfare are mighty to the pulling down of strongholds! The effectual fervent prayers of a righteous man availeth much (James 5:16)! Love is the key!

CHALLENGE
The World Coming to the Church!

The people in the World are hurting, lost, damaged, abused, addicts, suicidal, depressed, disoriented and confused just to name a few. They have tried everything else! They are coming to the Church/Spiritual Hospital for help!

When the World comes to the church and finds envying and strife, they will also find there is confusion and every evil work (James 3:16). The Lord said He has loved us with an everlasting love: therefore, with lovingkindness has He drawn us (Jeremiah 31:3). This is the only way we can draw the World. Love is what it does! The Lord said if He be lifted up from the earth, He will draw all men unto Him (John 12:32). Lift up Jesus by Praising Him and living a life that is pleasing to Him. You may be the only bible some people read. Your life should reflect the Christ you serve.

The Word of God instructs us to be transformed by the renewing of our mind that we may prove what is that good, acceptable and perfect will of God (Romans 12:2). If the World does not find this in the church, why should they want to come and stay. Why would the World want to attend services, pay tithes and offerings, and go to hell? There must be a difference!

The people come in one way in the church and leave the same way they came in. They come in with suicidal thoughts and leave with suicidal thoughts. They come in feeling depressed and leave depressed. They come in with hatred in their hearts and leave the same way. This ought not be! It is time for a change! There must be a change! It is Praying Time! It is Fasting Time! It is time for deliverance! Need More Word and More Jesus!

When the World does not find the wisdom that is from above that is first pure, then peaceable, gentle and easy to be intreated, full of mercy and good fruits, without partiality, and without hypocrisy and the fruit of righteousness sown in peace of them that make peace (James 3:16-18), the World will leave because there is no difference in the World and the Church. There must be a difference! There must be a change!

Don't get it twisted: The Word says, if we having a form of godliness, but denying the power thereof: from such turn away (2 Timothy 3:5). There must be a difference. We must proclaim/preach the Good News about Jesus who came to save the lost. We must live a holy and righteous life to draw others. It is time out for a "form of godliness"! We can spot phonies and so can the world. You are not fooling them. Stop playing games. Be real! We are talking about soul salvation. Heaven or Hell! Let us be an example of the Christ we talk and preach about. This is serious! This is judgment work! Be real! Be saved! Be sanctified! Be holy!

The World must find the fruits of the spirit which are love, joy, peace, long suffering, gentleness, goodness, faith, meekness, temperance (Galatians 5:22-23) or they might as well go back into the World for there is no difference. There must be a difference!

Our sin separates us from God and have hid God's face from us and He will not hear us (Isaiah 59:2). Let us be meet for the master's use. Let us be an example of Christ. Let your life reflect Christ in all you say and do!

The World we live in is hurting! We as God's ambassadors must fast and pray so that "this kinds" can be changed. We that are called by His name must humble ourselves, seek God's face and turn from our wicked ways, then we would hear from heaven and God will forgive our sins and will heal our land (2 Chronicles 7:14).

The effectual fervent prayers of a righteous man avails much. It is time to live a holy and righteous life! It is time to avail much for all our loved ones and others that we stand in the gap and pray for! We must live so that we can get a prayer through! You never know who you may have to pray for! Be ready! Stay prayerful! Pray without ceasing (1 Thessalonians 5:17).

IT IS BETTER THAT THE WORLD KNOWS YOU AS A SINNER THAN GOD KNOW YOU AS A HYPOCRITE or BLIND GUIDE (Matthew 29:23-24).

CHALLENGE
A Void In Your Life

Do you find yourself feeling lonely, frustrated, feeling like no one cares, feeling abandoned, disconnected, feel like you Need a boy or girl friend, don't know <u>what</u> to do, feel like no one understands you, feel like everyone is against you and feel like you are neglected? This is because you have a void in your life. You feel empty. The emptiness is trying to take hold of your mind, heart, soul and spirit. Many people have tried to fill that void with sex, drugs, alcohol, etc. trying to feel comforted; trying to feel satisfied; trying to find peace, love, joy, happiness; trying to feel complete and trying to feel comfortable.

God creates/allows a void in you that only He can fill. After you have suffered or gone through so many things, He will make you perfect, stablish, strengthen and settle you. There is a purpose for everything that you go through. We must acquaint ourselves with Him and be at peace; thereby good shall come unto you (Job 22:21).

All things work together for good to them that love God, to them who are the called according to His purpose (Romans 8:28). The Lord will perfect that which concerns you. His mercy endures forever (Psalm 138:8). Let God fill you up until you overflow!

God won't force Himself on you but will stand at the door of your heart and knock, if you humble yourself, pray, seek Him, turn from your wicked ways, then you will hear from heaven and He will forgive your sins and will heal you (2 Chronicles 7:14).

If you will hear His voice and open your heart, He will come into your heart and will dwell with you and Him with you (Revelation 3:20). His word shall not return Him void but it shall accomplish that which He please and shall prosper in the thing where He sent it (Isaiah 55:11). If you believe, there shall be a performance of those things which God has spoken to you through His word (Luke 1:45) and sometimes spoken to your heart.

Jesus says unto us "come unto me all that labor and are heavy laden and I will give you rest. Take my yoke upon you and learn of me; for I am meek and lowly in heart: and you shall find rest unto your souls (Matthew 11:28-29). Jesus cares about us and wants us to cast all our cares upon Him because He cares for us (1 Peter 5:7). We are instructed in the Word to cast our burdens upon the Lord, and He shall sustain us (Palms 55:22a). You must let go of the cares of this world or be bound in your daily walk! Let Go and Let God have it all! God can maintain and sustain you! He's Able to Deliver you from whatever is binding you or holding you down!

Jesus loves you so much that He suffered the death of the cross to redeem and reconcile you to Him. You feel empty when you are disconnected from your source of Power. Jesus is your source of Power. You were created to serve Him. The Word tells us that by God were all things created, that are in heaven, and that are in earth, visible and invisible, whether they be thrones, or dominions, or principalities, or powers: all things were created by him, and for him: (Colossians 1:16-17). Do not be deceived: the earth is the Lord's and the fulness thereof, the world, and they that dwell therein (Psalm 24:1). Everything belongs to God!

You can purchase an iron for $500 but if it is not plugged in, it has no power and it serves no purpose. Without a working power source, the iron is just an appliance with no real purpose because it cannot fulfill its purpose for which it was made. Power is needed to perform its task for which it was made. When you are disconnected from your source, Christ, you have no power working in you (Ephesians 3:20).

Our God is able to do exceedingly abundantly above all that we ask or think according to the power that works "in us". You must have a relationship with God to live a holy and righteous life in this world. It is imperative to your salvation and to fill the void in your life.

You must stay connected to Christ 24/7 to obtain the Power you need to fulfill your purpose, for which you were called and chosen by God, to fulfill even before the foundation of the world. You were chosen before the foundation of the world that you should be holy and without blame before Him in love (Ephesians1:4).

You must follow/pursue peace with everyone and live a holy/clean life for if you are not holy, we will not see the

Lord. All the hell we have had to live with in this world and then go to hell is like 2 times. You get to choose which way you want to live and die. You can live any kind of way you want (good or bad) but you better not die unholy. It is your choice! Choose you this day who you will serve. If God be God, then serve Him.

There is peace in Jesus. There is comfort in Jesus. There is love in and with Jesus. There is joy and peace in Jesus. There is power and strength in Jesus. There is healing and deliverance in Jesus. You must look to Jesus who is the author and finisher of your faith (Hebrews 12:2a).

Jesus could not do many mighty works/ miracles because of unbelief (Matthew 13:58). We must believe that He is, and He is a rewarder of them that diligently seek Him (Hebrews 11:6). Be not afraid, only believe for all things are possible if you only believe. The Word instructs us to seek first the kingdom of God and His righteousness and all things shall be added unto us. If you seek God, you will find Him. If you keep your mind stayed Him, He will give you perfect peace. The Lord will give you peace (Numbers 6:26b). The Lord will supply all your need according to His riches in glory by Christ Jesus (Philippians 4:19). Keep your mind on Jesus to keep perfect peace!

It is so important to have a relationship with God. Let Jesus lead you and direct your path. Do not let others validate, define you or tell you what or how you are supposed to act! To thine own self be true! Be who God says you are. Praise God for you are fearfully and wonderfully made (Psalm 139:14a).

When you have a relationship with God, He will supply all your need (Philippians 4:19). Get to know Him for yourself; you will be at peace and good shall come unto you (Job 28:21). If you seek Him, He will give you revelation and wisdom   that the eyes of your understanding will be enlightened and you will know the hope of His calling, and what the riches of the glory of His inheritance in the saints (Ephesians 1:17-18). Seek Him while He may be found. Call upon Him while He is yet near. If you seek the Lord, you shall not want any good thing (Psalm 34:10b).

This one thing you should do, forget those things behind you and reach forth unto those things which are before and press towards the mark for the prize of the high calling in Christ Jesus (Philippians 3:14). Do not allow your past to dictate your future! Do not be afraid, dismayed or distressed by the many things that you go through. The battle is not yours. It's God's! (2 Chronicles 20:15).

God knows how to take care of His own. His hands are not shortened that it cannot save neither His ear heavy that it cannot hear you (Isaiah 59:1). Delight yourself (seek to live a life pleasing to Him) in the Lord and He shall give you the desires of your heart (Psalm 37:4).

CHALLENGE
The Trick of the Enemy

The enemy plants a thought in your mind and comes back frequently to harvest that thought (get you to think about it). Then tries to get you to say it out your mouth what he put in your thought so you can call things that are not into existence! Don't get it twisted! The devil knows the word. There was a war in heaven. He was cast out of heaven along with his angels. You must put on the whole armour of God so that you will be able to stand against the wiles (luring, enticing, trickery and persuasion) of the devil (Ephesians 6:11).

You have to hide God's word in your heart so that you might not sin against Him. You continue to fight in your mind saying no that is not me or ever will be me! He keeps coming at you to say it! Do not say it! From out of the abundance of the heart, the mouth speaks! You try to ignore it and it keeps coming back. You have to Deal with it, or it will continue to try and deal with you.

You have to cast down all your imaginations and every high thing that exalts itself against the knowledge of God and ask God to bring your every thought into captivity to the obedience of Christ (2 Corinthians 10:5). This is one of the weapons of warfare that you must use to be victorious over the enemy. You must actively fight to maintain God's vision and purpose for you. If the thoughts that come into your mind do not line up with the Word of God, you must not accept it.

Let God have it all! God can give you perfect peace. Set your affection on things above, not on things on the earth (Colossians 3:2). Use your weapons: 1) bind and rebuke the thoughts back to the pit of hell from where it came and 2) plead the blood of Jesus over your heart, mind, body, soul, spirit and thoughts. There's power in the blood to break every chain. The blood still works! It reaches to the highest mountain and flows to the lowest valley. It will never ever lose its power!

We have to be careful to not become spoiled (to cause to decay and perish) by others through philosophy and vain deceit, after the tradition of men, after the rudiments (undeveloped or imperfect form of something) of the world, and not after Christ (Colossians 2:8).

God has promised us that if we trust and keep our mind on Him that He would keep us in perfect peace (Isaiah 26:3). Always be sober, be vigilant, because the adversary, the devil, as a roaring lion, walks about seeking whom he may devour (destroy completely) (1Peter 5:8). The devil wants to destroy you completely by any means necessary. If he has to use your mind against you, he will definitely try.

You must remain stedfast, unmovable, always abounding in the work of the Lord, for as much as you know that your labor is not in vain in the Lord (1 Corinthians 15:58). Stay connected to the power of God or become disconnected and be used by the enemy to destroy you!

The Word says be careful for nothing; but in everything by prayer and supplication with thanksgiving let your requests be made known unto God and the peace of God, which passes all understanding, shall keep your hearts and minds through Christ Jesus (Philippians 4:6-7). Prayer (sincere thanksgiving or requests made to God), supplications (form of prayer but considered as kneeling/bending down in which someone makes a humble petition to God) with thanksgiving is absolutely necessary for your heart and mind to be kept by Christ.

Christ makes intercession for you (Romans 8:34c). He prays and ask/petitions of God for you. Christ is able to save you to the uttermost that come to God by Him. He lives to make intercession for you (Hebrews 7:25).

Commit your works unto the Lord and your thoughts shall be established (Proverbs 16:3). The confidence that we have in Christ is that if we ask any thing according to His will, He hears us. And if we know that He hears us, whatsoever we ask, we know that we have the petitions that we desired of Him (1 John 5:14-15). A relationship with Christ is mandatory to avoid the tricks of the enemy.

Be who God says you are! You are born again, redeemed, restored, revived and renewed in the spirit of your mind; You have to gird up the loins of your mind, be sober, and hope to the end for the grace that is to be brought unto you at the revelation of Jesus Christ (1 Peter 1:13).

You are not who the enemy says you are! Continue to read your Word and pray! God's Word says that He will keep you in perfect peace, if your mind is stayed on Him, because you trust in Him. The enemy will try to have your mind wandering. An idle mind is the devil's workshop (2 Timothy 2:6). Sometimes you have to make a conscious effort to keep your mind stayed on godly things and not the cares of this world.

Praise is an extraordinarily strong weapon of warfare. God inhabits the praises of His people (Psalm 22:3). The Word says let your mouth be filled with your praise and your honor all day (Psalm 71:8). Praise Him in all things, good or bad because you know He is in control. The song says, when praises go up, blessings come down, healing and deliverance comes down. From the rising of the sun unto the going down of the same the Lord's name is to be praised (Psalm 113:3). Praise God until you get a breakthrough. Don't wait until the battle is over! Shout now! You know in the end, you win! For of Him, and through Him, and to Him, are all things: to whom be glory forever (Romans 11:36)

The enemy is doing what he told God he would do. The devil is walking about, seeking who he can devour. (1 Peter 5:8). We have to do what Jesus did for a foul spirit that tried to take over a person. Jesus rebuked the foul spirit and "charged it to come out and enter no more" (Mark 9:25). You must charge every foul spirit to come out and enter you no more in Jesus name! Believe to receive! It is so! We are the redeemed of the Lord and we say so, for He has redeemed us from the hand of the enemy (Psalm 107:2). We are redeemed and we say So!

When you know that your mind belongs to God then the enemy has to try another trick! The word instructs us to let the mind be in us which was also in Christ Jesus. We have to change the way we think and talk. Our conversations should reflect the mind of Christ and not the former conversation of the sinful man which is corrupt (Ephesians 4:22a). You must be renewed in the spirit of your mind. Put on the new man, which after God is created in righteousness and true holiness (Ephesians 4:22-24). You must continue to be stedfast, unmovable, always abounding in the work of the Lord, then you know that your labor is not in vain in the Lord (1 Corinthians15:58)!

You do not want your labor to be in vain. You do not want your fasting, praying, going to church, reading God's word and trying to live right to be in vain. By continuing to be stedfast, unmovable and always abounding the work of the Lord will protect and keep you from the tricks of the enemy.

God won't let you down! You are a vessel of honor! Meet for the Master's use! You must not be conformed to this world: but you must be transformed by the renewing of your mind, that you may prove that good, acceptable, and perfect will of God (Romans 12:2). You must not allow yourself to act in any way different than what the Word of God teaches or your character to change from who God says you are. If it does not align itself with the Word of God, then you must separate yourself if possible, or ask God to keep you in the midst of it all. Our God is Awesome! He won't fail you! Your mind must be transformed to God's will, way, plan and purpose for your life! Forever our God rules and reigns!

CHALLENGE
Love Through It All (Spiritual Stand)

Let this day be the first day of the beginning of the rest of your life. Jesus loves us so much! Jesus came the way that He did to let us know that we can make it through any obstacle, sickness, suffering, problem, trial, tribulation, circumstance or situation. You can make it with Christ on your side. His mercy endures forever, and His compassion never fails.

From being carried by a humble virgin girl; a barn as a birthing room; laying in a manger; living the humble life; walking about being about His Father's business; arrested, beaten, slapped, ridiculed, forsaken by God for us, mocked, pierced in His side, nailed to the cross by His hands and feet, hung for our sins, died and went and got the key from hell for us and in 3 days Jesus rose with all power in His hands! Now that's love!

There is power in the name of Jesus to break every chain and tear down every stronghold. For God so loved us that He gave His Son and His Son gave His life for us! Now that's love!

No greater love hath no man than this for us! Love is one of the greatest weapons of our warfare to bring down strongholds! Love is so powerful it covers a multitude of sin (1 Peter 4:8). Love binds wounds. Love heals. Love cares. Love never gives up. Jesus loved us even when we didn't love ourselves or others.

Let's love more and show it more! The more love you have in you, the more God you have in you because God is love! Love and care! They must go together! Love heals your heart and sets your spirit free! One of the keys to peace and longevity is forgiveness. You must forgive and be set free from past hurts and wounds. If you forgive, then your heavenly Father will also forgive you, but if you don't forgive others neither will God forgive you (Matthew 6:14-15).

Love your enemies; those that despitefully used you: those that lied on you and those you can't stand. We are commanded to love one another (John 15:12). The Word also instructs us to let all our things be done with charity. Charity is love (1 Corinthians 16:1). We know and believe the love that God has for us. God is love and if you dwell in love then you dwell in God and God dwells in you (1 John 4:16). We have faith, hope and charity, but the greatest of these is charity/love (1 Corinthians 13:13). Love is a powerful weapon of warfare.

God loved the world so much that He gave His only begotten Son for us that believe in Him that we shall not perish but have everlasting life (John 3:16). No man hath seen God at any time. If we love one another, then God dwells in us and His love is perfected in us (1 John 4:12). We need perfect love because it cast out fear (1 John 4:18).

Let's be like Jesus and stop being selfish! Jesus was a lover and giver! He loved and He gave His life for us! Let's have the same mind. Let's stand for something or we will fall for anything! Stand for Christ and He will stand for you! Depart from Him and He will depart from you! Return to Him and He will return to you! Remain in Him and He will Remain in you!

Love not because of but in spite of! Remember we don't wrestle against flesh and blood but against principalities (demonic rulers), against the rulers of the darkness of this world, against spiritual wickedness in high places (Ephesians 6:12). You must have a forgiving heart. You must let it go! Christ Jesus disarmed the powers and authorities,

He made a public spectacle of them, triumphing over them by the cross (Colossians 2:15 NIV).

God loved us so He gave His only begotten Son, Christ Jesus, that whosoever believes in Him should not perish, but have everlasting life (John 3:16). Because He loved us so much, Christ suffered death for us. He was made lower than the angels for a little while and was crowned with glory and honor because He suffered death for us. By the grace of God, He tasted death for everyone (Hebrews 2:9 NIV).

Let all your things be done with charity (love) 1 Corinthians 16:14. If you don't love, you don't know God, for God is love (1 John 4:8). The new commandment He gave us is that we love one another as He loved us so that you should also love another. By our love for love another, everyone shall know that we are Christ's disciples if we have love one to another (John 13:34-35). Let us love one another: for love is of God; and every one that loves is born of God and knows God (1

John 4 :7). It may be hard to love those that have lied on you, treated you badly, despitefully used you, stolen from you, took away your dignity and even now are not sorry for what they did. Let it go! Let God do what He does best. Be God! He does not want us to avenge ourselves.

Vengeance belongs to God. For God has said, He will repay! He will take care of it and them. He said don't be deceived, God is not mocked for whatsoever a man sows/does, he shall also reap/receive (Galatians 6:7). It comes back around. You will see it again!

Remember love is patient, love is kind, it does not envy, it does not boast, it is not proud. It does not dishonor others, it is not self-seeking, it is not easily angered, it keeps no record of wrongs. Love does not delight in evil but rejoices with the truth. It always protects, always trusts, always hopes, always perseveres. Love never fails. There are three things that remain; faith, hope and love but the greatest of these is love (1 Corinthians 13:4-8, 13 NIV).

Love not because of but in spite of what has been done to you, It's time to Stop Spiritual Stagnation because someone hurt your feelings or treated you wrongly. You are More Than A Conqueror!

Let us remember that at one time we too were foolish, disobedient, deceived and enslaved by all kinds of passions and pleasures. We lived in malice and envy, hated and hated one another but when the kindness and love of God our Savior appeared, He saved us, not because of our righteous things we had done, but because of His mercy. He saved us through the washing of rebirth and renewal by the Holy Spirit, whom He poured out on us generously through Jesus Christ our Savior. So that, being justified by His grace, we might become heirs having the hope of eternal life. These things are being stressed so that those who have trusted in

God may be careful to devote themselves to doing what is good. These things are excellent and profitable to everyone (Titus 3:3-8 NIV). In all these things we are more than conquerors through Him that loved us (Romans 8:37).

The secret to being free is not holding onto things of the past or revenge but letting things go. Free your mind! Free your heart! Concentrate on making the next chapter of your life the best of your life. So, believe, love, smile, laugh, forgive and be the best you that you can be!

CHALLENGE
Your Mind

The enemy of our soul comes to steal, to kill and to destroy! Steal your peace of mind! Having you thinking on things that are not of God or of you! Stealing your sane mind right in front of you! Steal your joy, love, compassion, righteousness, hope, faith, redemption, your right to the tree of life, trust and obedience and holiness by drawing you away by your own lust! Steal your connection and relationship with Christ by robbing you of time needed to pray! Causing problems and distractions to lure you away from who you are in Christ. Even having you speaking defeat over your own lives! To kill you by using you!

You are given to appetite and destroying your desire to seek God because of what you have gone through! The enemy of your soul wants to kill you while you are in a moment of weakness and unbelief! Just remember, God said He would keep you in perfect peace if your mind is stayed on Him! Keep a prayer on your heart and a song on your mind.

When you have a peace of mind, you have joy! Joy in spite of what's going on around you. The joy of the Lord is your strength (Nehemiah 8:10d).

Jesus came that we might have life and to have it more abundantly! Pray and ask God to pour more of Him into you; to give you a fresh anointing to break that curse that has infected your mind, body, soul and spirit that you were not aware of!

Pray and ask God to help you. He will! Ask Him to please don't allow the past hurts to kill your future happiness; to please don't allow the suffering you had to endure in the past to destroy your present peace; and to please help you to not eat those things that hurt or destroy your temple/organs!

We have not because we ask not. Believe and ask to receive according to God's divine will, way, plan and purpose for your life. What? Know you not that your body is a temple of the Holy Ghost which is in you, which you have of God, and you are not your own (1 Corinthians 6:19). For you are bought with a price: therefore, glorify God in your body, and in your spirit (1 Corinthians 6:20).

You must seek deliverance from the thief that has snook up in your house! Once you become knowledgeable of the tricks of the enemy, you will become stronger because you know that God is with you and goes before and with you. God said He would never fail you nor forsake you (Deuteronomy 31:6b).

God is our refuge and a very present help in the time of trouble (Psalm 46:1). The thief is watching and waiting for your moment of weakness! 1 Peter 5:8-9 instructs us to be sober, be vigilant; because the adversary the devil, as a roaring lion, walketh about, seeking whom he may devour: and you are to resist stedfast in your faith, knowing that the same afflictions are accomplished in your brethren that are in the world. You are not alone.

Many are the afflictions of the righteous, but the Lord delivers us out of them all (Psalm 34:19). When God is for you, who can be against us (Romans 3:31b). He is more than the whole world against you. Greater is He that is in you than he that is in the world (1 John 4:4b! In all these things, you are more than a conqueror through Him that loved us (Romans 8:37).

The saints are under attack by the thief! The thief tries to attack the mind to cripple the body. You must keep your mind on Jesus and not get caught up with the cares of this world. You can have perfect peace in your mind if you trust in God. God said He would keep us in perfect peace if our mind is stayed on Him because we trust in Him (Isaiah 26:3).

The weapons of your warfare are mighty through the pulling down of strongholds (2 Corinthians 10:4). The kingdom of heaven suffers violence and the violent taketh by force! (Matthew 11:12). Jesus is our lethal weapon! In the time of attack, the name of Jesus is a strong tower (Proverbs 18:10)! Jesus is our battle axe in the time of trouble (Jeremiah 51:20)!

If you linger in your revisiting remembrances of your past hurts, they can actually reinjure your mind, heart, soul and spirit if you do not get your focus back on Christ and let it go! The past belongs to the Lord.

When memories of the past come to haunt you in your present, you must ask God to remove those thoughts from your heart! When you allow memories to linger in your mind, they will take root in your heart again and then it's hard to be released from your mind, soul and spirit! You must go to God, the author and finisher of your faith and allow Him to create in you a clean heart and renew a right spirit within you.

The enemy desires to keep you bound in the past so that you can't hardly do anything towards the upbuilding of God's kingdom. Turn it over to Jesus. Jesus will work it out for you! God said He would keep you in perfect peace if your mind was stayed on Him. Keep your mind stayed on Jesus! Keep a prayer on your mind! Keep a song in your spirit! Keep a praise in your mouth! Keep your soul worshipping Him! Keep your will under subjection of the Holy Ghost! Keep a Word in your heart! When you do this, you are guarding your spirit! You must guard your spirit at all times! You must have rule over your own spirit (Proverbs 25:28).

The enemy tries to bind the saints with personal problems, situations, illnesses, troubles so the church can never grow because the families are bound with personal problems. God said cast all your cares upon Him because He cares for us. Our God is Awesome! Our God is greater than any pain, cancer, problems or anything that comes your way. When the enemy presents his stuff, just say, Jesus will You get that for me. Let God be the Master of your everything! He will come through for you!

The greater you is waiting to come forth and fulfill your purpose that God called and chose you for even before the foundation of the world! Come Forth! Do not be bound by the past in Jesus name! Trust and believe that it is So!

Trouble don't last always! Weeping may endure for a night, keep the faith, it will be alright! Joy cometh in the morning! In God's presence is fullness of joy! Just bask in His presence and the anointing will destroy every yoke. Every yoke shall be broken in Jesus name! Every promise will be fulfilled! God will come through!

You must not be conformed/agree to this world but be transformed/changed by the renewing of your mind that you may prove what is that good, acceptable and perfect will of God (Romans 12:2). The god of this world has blinded the minds of them which believe not so that the light of the glorious gospel of Christ, who is the image of God, should shine unto them (2 Corinthians 4:4).

Without faith it is impossible to please God. For if you come to God, you must believe that God is and that He is a rewarder of them that diligently seek Him. If you seek God, you will find Him when you shall search for Him with all your heart (Jeremiah 29:13). Call unto Him!

Finally, whatsoever things are true, whatsoever things are honest, whatsoever things are just, whatsoever things are pure, whatsoever things are lovely, whatsoever things are of good report; if there be any virtue, and if there be any praise, think on these things (Philippians 4:8).

CHALLENGE
Your Heart

Your Natural Heart is an organ that pumps blood throughout the body. Your Spiritual Heart includes your intellect, emotion and free will. Your Spiritual Heart consists of so many things. In your Spiritual Heart you examine or have regard to things. Thou shalt also consider in thine heart (Deuteronomy 8:5a). You have knowledge in your heart. You can pray in your heart as Hannah did (1 Samuel 1:12-13). You can pray and meditate in your heart. Let the words of my mouth, and the meditation of my heart, be acceptable in thy sight, O LORD, my strength, and my redeemer (Psalm 19:14).

It is very important to have a constant prayer relationship with God. Through maintaining our prayer relationship with

God, He will keep our hearts, words and lives free from sin and thereby pleasing to Him. We do this by hiding God's word in our hearts (Psalm 110:11). We try to reason things within our hearts (Mark 2:8). We must trust God, lean not unto our own understanding, but in all our ways acknowledge Him and He shall direct our paths (Proverbs 3:5-6). The traits involve inner knowing. It's so very important to maintain a personal relationship with God.

The Spiritual Heart is also a center of feeling. In the heart, you can be glad (Exodus 4:14a). You can have a loving heart (Deuteronomy 6:5). You can also have a fearful heart (Joshua 5:1). You can have a courageous heart (Psalm 27:14). These are a few traits that involve the inner feeling of the heart.

The Spiritual Heart is also the faculty or power of using one's will. You can have a hardened heart that refuses to do what God commands (Exodus 4:21). You can have a heart that yields to God (Joshua 24:23). You can have a heart that desires to receive from the Lord (Psalm 21:1-2). You can also have a heart that is devoted to seeking the Lord (1 Chronicles 22:19) to name a few. These traits primarily take place in the human will.

You must guard/keep your heart, or the very cares of this world will rob you of all you are called to be! Your love and compassion for your fellow man will be lost in the pains and hurts you suffered by the hands of others! Keep your heart with all diligence, for out it are the issues of life (Proverbs 4:23). Guard (watch over it) your heart for everything you do flows from it! Jesus said, those things which proceed out of the mouth come forth from the heart, and they defile the man. For out of the heart proceed evil thoughts, murders, adulteries, fornications, thefts, false witness and blasphemies (Matthew 15:18-19). You must keep your mind focused on Jesus or be lost.

Be not deceived: evil communications corrupt good manners (1 Corinthians 15:33). You must not be so motivated by the need to be accepted that you allow your Godly wisdom in making decisions to be persuaded by peer pressure or ungodly influences that may corrupt our heart, mind, soul and spirt. You must stand firm against those who would corrupt your walk with Christ. You must watch as well as pray that you enter not into temptation: the spirit is willing, but the flesh is weak (Matthew 26:41). You must be careful for nothing; but in everything by prayer and supplication with thanksgiving let your requests be made known unto God (Philippians 4:6). Each day, you must seek God to create in you a clean heart and renew a right spirit within you (Psalm 51:10).

Be strong and courageous for the Lord is always with you and will never leave you nor forsake you! Don't let somebody else define who you are! Don't let somebody else's problems, situations, circumstances define how you should feel about an issue! Don't let somebody else's failures define who you are! Don't let somebody else tell you what direction to follow.

To guard/keep your heart, you must study to shew thyself approved, a workman that need not be ashamed, rightly dividing the Word of Truth (2 Timothy 2:15). The cares of this world will blind you as to who you were called to be! That which is precious to you, guard it! God always provides a way out for us! We must equip ourselves!

Don't get it twisted, the enemy comes to kill, steal and destroy everything you stand for (your love, joy, peace and spiritual growth)! Jesus came that you might have life and have it more abundantly (John 10:10).

To guard/keep your heart, you have to cast down imaginations, and every high thing that exalts itself against the knowledge of God and ask God to bring into captivity your every thought to the obedience of Christ (2 Corinthians 10:5).

The peace of God, which passes all understanding, shall keep your hearts and minds through Christ Jesus (Philippians 4:7). You must sanctify the Lord God in your hearts: and be ready always to give an answer to every man that asks you a reason of the hope that is in you with meekness and fear (1 Peter 3:15).

Seek God while He may be found! Call upon Him while He is yet near (Isaiah 55:6)! Watch and pray that you enter not into temptation for the spirit indeed is willing, but the flesh is weak (Matthew 26:41).

The Spirit also helps our infirmities: for we know not what we should pray for as we ought: but the Spirit itself makes intercession for us with groanings which cannot be uttered

(Romans 8:26). Now the Lord is that Spirit and where the Spirit of the Lord is, there is liberty (2 Corinthians 3:17).

DO NOT BE DECEIVED: Blessed are the pure in heart: for they shall see God. A pure hearted person has no hidden motives and is not a gossiper. Your desire will be to please God in all things. To get a clean/pure heart, we must do as Psalm 51:10 says, "Create in me a clean (pure) heart, O God, and renew a right spirit within me."

God is not okay with you doing evil things to others even if they did evil to you! We are to resist the devil and he will flee! If you have a clean heart, you will treat people right. You won't put others down! The only time you would look down on others would be to lift them up! With a clean heart, you will love others even if they don't love you back.

CHALLENGE
Fake Christians

There is no such thing as a Fake Christian! If you are a Christian, then you are Christ like. To be Christ like is to portray characteristics of Christ. Fake is counterfeit. So, you can't be a Fake Christian. You are just a liar and a phony. Fooling no one, not even yourself! It's just a form of Godliness denying the power thereof (2 Timothy 3:5)! You can't serve two Masters! God will not have you lukewarm, and neither cold nor hot! He said He would spue you out His mouth (Revelation 3:16).

Choose you this Day who you will serve. If God be God, then serve Him with your whole heart, mind, soul and spirit. Be

Real! God is watching you! You are writing your life story! Be who He called you to be!

You can either live for Jesus or die and go to hell. It's your choice! Choose Life or Death! Where will your final destiny place be above or beneath? Heaven or hell? You choose!

CHALLENGE
Happiness, Joy and Peace

Are you seeking happiness, joy or peace? Happiness, joy and peace is not outside of you or in other people. It is in you. It's you! You are happiness, joy and peace. You feel alone? Just not happy? If you can't be happy with you, why seek somebody else to make you happy! When they don't make you happy then you are even sadder. Why would you think somebody else would be happy with you if you are not happy with yourself?

Happy is the man that finds wisdom, and the man that gets understanding (Proverbs 3:13). Whoso trusts in the Lord, happy is he (Proverbs 16:20b). Rejoice in the Lord always: and again, I say, Rejoice (Philippians 4:4)! The joy of the Lord is your strength (Nehemiah 8:10d). A merry heart does good like medicine (Proverbs 17:22). God makes each day and you should rejoice and be glad in it (Psalm 118:24).

Seek ye first the kingdom of God, and His righteousness and all these things will be added unto you (Matthew 6:33). God can fill any void in your life. Oh, He makes you happy! And oh, the joy He brings and the peace of mind knowing that the Almighty is watching over you 24/7.

The eyes of the Lord are upon the righteous, and His ears are open unto their cry. The righteous cry, and the Lord hears and delivers them out of all their troubles (Psalm 34:15, 17).

Spend some quality time with God. Get to know who God says you are. Take a walk with Him through His word. Let Him reveal mysteries upon mysteries to you on your journey through the word. The peace of God passes all understanding shall keep your heart and mind through Christ Jesus (Philippians 4:7).

You must love you and care about you. Treat you right! Don't let anyone define you or validate you. Be you! Be the best you that you can be! Be all God says or calls you to be!

Guard your heart and don't let other people think they can control you, dictate to you or make them think that you need them to be happy! Be happy unto yourself! Delight yourself in the Lord and He shall give you the desires of your heart (Psalm 37:4).

In the presence of God is fullness of joy (Psalm 16:11). God is the portion of your inheritance (Psalm 16:5). He hears our prayer and supplication and maintains our cause (1 Kings 8:45). The thoughts that God thinks towards us, saith the Lord, are thoughts of peace, and not evil, to give us an expected end (Jeremiah 29:11). God has plans to prosper you and not harm you; plans to give you hope and a future. You may not know what your future holds but when you know who holds your future, you can rejoice!

When you choose Christ as your savior, you will have peace in the midst of a storm. The God of hope will fill you with all joy and peace in believing, that you may abound in hope through the power of the Holy Ghost. We have not seen God, but we love Him yet believing, we rejoice with joy unspeakable and full of glory (1 Peter 1:8).

God will keep you in perfect peace if your mind is stayed on Him because we trust in Him (Isaiah 26:3). The Lord will give you perfect peace if your faith is firm. Hold fast the profession of your faith without wavering for God is faithful to His promises (Hebrews 10:23),

You can have perfect peace in all things! God shall direct your paths if you trust in Him with all your heart, lean not unto your own understanding and in all your ways acknowledge Him (Proverbs 3:5-6).

If you don't have joy, rejoice and leap for it (Luke 6:23a)! Happiness, joy and peace are yours for the asking. If you ask, it shall be given; seek, and you shall find; knock, and it shall be opened unto you. For everyone that asks receives; and to him that knocks it shall be opened (Matthew 7:7-8). God has granted you access to fulfil your needs. It's up to you to ask Him! Be happy! Be joyful! Be at peace! It's your treasure but you must open it!

CHALLENGE
Your Life Story

If you could ever write your life story, what would you want to leave as a legacy for your family and friends! Would you leave your favorite scripture to live by? What encouraging words would you leave?

If you could ever write your life story, what would you like to be remembered by (your life, your talk, your jokes, your position or title in life, your love for others, your support of the underprivileged, your laughter). What would you write? What are you writing?

Each awakening day is another line in your story! Each day is the today of yesterday. You are writing into the Book of

Life right now! Are you okay with what you are writing? Is there something you might want to change? Think about it!

God gave you today so love, not because of but in spite of! Forgive so you can be forgiven. If you don't forgive others neither will God forgive you (Matthew 6:15). Forgive to live abundantly and grow spiritually! Unforgiveness robs you of the fullness of your life. Let it go!

Repent, return to God and remain in Him so you can be renewed, revived, restored, redeemed and reconciled back to Him! Don't let your tomorrows slip up on your today for the last writing of you in the Book of Your Life! And if you are not in the Book of Life... Well.... Don't be blotted out of the Book of Life!

Don't be your circumstance! Don't be your situation or problem! Don't be someone else's slave. Don't allow yourself to be used! My Mom always told me, no one does any more to you than you let them. Know who you are and stand up for what you believe. Don't be blinded by things. You get to choose what type of person you want to be and the impact you want to leave on others. Don't let where you come from determine who you are or where you are going! This is your story! You get to write the paragraphs in each chapter. You choose!

Wisdom says treat others the way you want to be treated. That way others can never hold power over you because you are who God says you are! Take the pressure off yourself and turn things over to God. Give God control and let Him take your bad yesterdays and change you into a revived, restored and renewed vessel of honor. Forgive often and love with all your heart. Learn to release your burdens to the Lord.

The Word says cast your cares upon the Lord. You must learn to be a Spiritual disciple by practicing your faith by studying your bible. By reading/studying your bible, it opens a doorway to a deeper relationship with God. Rather than focus on the problem, you can instead focus on the problem solver. Go from being defined by others and be refined by the Word of God.

Our task is to surrender our lives to Christ and let Him work through us! The Power of God gives us a greater measure of boldness and defense against whatever we face. God will restore, confirm, strengthen and establish you (I Peter 5:10).

Let your life reflect who you serve! Your walk should reflect who holds your future! Your talk should reflect who lives in your heart! Be Who God says you are! Be true to yourself or be stagnated or blinded by what others think of you.

Situations, sickness, circumstances, problems, people or trials are part of the journey but that's not who you are!!

Don't allow something or someone to dictate or define who you are! Do not allow someone to persuade you to do or say anything that doesn't reflect who you are! Be Who God Says You Are! To thine own self, be true!

You were called and chosen before the foundation of the world with a purpose! Ask God to help you to be so focused on your purpose that nothing or no one can move you from God's Divine Destiny for you! Do those things that are pleasing to God and be stedfast, unmovable in His Word so that your labor is not in vain!

Choose you this day who you will serve! Only the pure in heart shall see God!!

You must Let Go of hurtful past experiences and not allow them to choose what kind of person you are or will become. You get to choose! Choose you this day who you will serve.

Let Jesus come into your heart and make and mold you into the person for whom you were created or born to be. You were born for God's divine purpose. Choose Now for Today and for All Your Tomorrows!

Choose God's divine will, way, plan and purpose for your life! You may not know what your future holds but you know who holds your future in the palm of His hands!

CHALLENGE
Forgiveness

THINK ABOUT IT: If you forgive then your heavenly Father will forgive you but if you don't forgive others neither will He forgive you (Matthew 6:14-15)! Forgive and set yourself free! Free to love with no boundaries. Free to serve God to the uttermost. Free to live a holy and righteous life!

Your Forgiveness of others is the first step to Your Spiritual Elevation! Stop holding yourself back from your own blessings! Nothing happens unless God allows it! If there are evil thoughts against you, God means it for your good (Genesis 50:20)! All things (bad things too) shall work together for your good (Romans 8:28)

It's a Challenge but Love your enemies and do good to them which hate you (Luke 6:27). Hatred stirs up strifes, but love covers all sins.

It's Time for Forgiveness! When you don't forgive someone, you give them power over you! Forgiveness is for you! Forgive
so that You Can Grow and Live Life to its Fullest! Most of All, Forgive Others so God will Forgive You!

Forgive so you can be what you want or need to be! Forgive so you can go where you want or need to go! Forgive so you get what you want or need to get'! Forgive so you see what you need to see! Forgive so you can accomplish what you need to accomplish!

2 Corinthians 2:10-11 says, To whom you forgive anything, I forgive also: for if I forgave anything, to whom I forgave it, for your sakes forgave I it in the person of Christ; Lest Satan

should get an advantage of us: for we are not ignorant of his devices. You must forgive to keep your power. A forgiving heart can reach God while a stagnated heart is bound to the cares of this world. Satan desires to sift you. Use your weapon of forgiveness to access God's love and protection for you and your loved ones.

When you stand praying, forgive, if you have ought against any: that your Father also which is in heaven may forgive you your trespasses (Mark 11:25). Let it go! Let Go and Let God Deliver You! Be kind one to another, tenderhearted, forgiving one another, even as God for Christ's sake has forgiven you (Ephesians 4:32).

Always forgive everyone in your past that hurt you, harm you, talked about you, put you down, lied on you, deceived you, didn't treat you the way you thought you should have been treated, handled you wrong, used you, persecuted you or scandalized your name! It doesn't matter what was said, let it go! It may have really embarrassed you, let it go! They may have put you down in front of others, let it go! Let Go and Let God deliver you from you!

Most importantly, you must forgive yourself! Forgive yourself for bad decisions, mistakes you made, whether real or imagined! Let God deliver you from you! Forgive yourself for not having the wisdom to make different choices in your life. Forgive yourself for allowing others to tell you what to think and do. Forgive yourself so that you can grow beyond and past anything that has you bound or stagnated.

CHALLENGE
Unconditional Love

God is love and those that know God, keep his commandments. The Scriptures says "love your enemies", "love those that despitefully use you"; "love your neighbor as yourself"; "treat others the way you want to be treated"; "do all that you do to the glory of God"; "whatsoever you sow, you shall reap"; etc. You have to hide God's word in your hearts so that you might not sin against Him (Psalm 119:11).

God loved us so much that He gave His only begotten Son that whosoever believes in Him should not perish but have everlasting life (John 3:16). No greater love hath no man than Jesus that He laid down His life for us (John 15:13). We love God because He first loved us (1 John 4:19).

If you don't love, you don't know God for God is love (1 John 4:8). We are to love one another because when you love you are born of God and know Him (1 John 4:7). Above all things, we are to have fervent love among ourselves for love shall cover the multitude of sins (1 Peter 4:8).

Jesus told us that the first and greatest commandment is to love the Lord our God with all our heart, soul and mind. And the second is to that we shall love our neighbor as our self (Matthew 22:36-39). We are commanded to love!

There is no fear in love. Perfect love casts out fear (1 John 4:18a). Love suffers long and is kind, envies not, vaunts not itself and is not puffed up. Love does not behave itself unseemly, seeks not its own, is not easily provoked and thinks no evil. Love rejoices not in iniquity, believes all things, hopes for all things and endures all things. Love never fails (1 Corinthians 13:4-8a). Love is forgiving!

If a person says he knows God and don't keep His commandments, he is a liar, and the truth is not in him (1 John 2:4). For the Word says there are many rebellious people, full of meaningless talk and deception, especially those of the circumcision group (Titus 1:10). They engage in useless talk and deceive others. Don't be deceived. We have to seek God for revelation and wisdom in knowing God so that the eyes of our understanding can be enlightened so we can know the hope of His calling and our inheritance as saints (Ephesians 1:18). Get to know God for yourself!

If you claim to know God, but by your actions you deny Him. You are being abominable and disobedient and unfit for doing anything good (Titus 1:16). Also, if we claim to have fellowship with God and yet walk in the darkness, we lie and do not live out the truth (1 John 1:6).

Whoever claims to love God yet hates a brother or sister is a liar. For whoever does not love their brother and sister whom they have seen, cannot love God whom they have not seen (1 John 4:20). We are commanded to love!

The one thing that the scripture does not say but should be understood is that don't let other people determine how you treat or love another! Get to know a person for yourself! In most cases, to know them is to love them!

So many times, people, family or church members have had a bad experience with another person, and they pass onto others their take on the situation and taint other people's thoughts, opinions or even love for them! Then for no reason at all, the person starts treating the other person cold! This ought not be especially among the saints! Thank God, Jesus loves us and knows whose we are!

Don't allow yourself to be stagnated by judgmental people that don't have anything else to do but talk about you or others! They talked about Jesus! They lied on Jesus! They whipped Him, spit in His face, crucified Him and He did no wrong! Small minded people talk about others hoping to put others down thereby elevating themselves!

Let Your Destination be Defined by God Alone Not Your Problems, Situations or Obstacles!

You should love one another, not because of, but in spite of all that has happened. Let all your things be done with love (1 Corinthians 16:14). Love your way through any problem. Love wins all the time! Don't allow how you were treated to change how you love. Remain stedfast and unmovable in loving and allow God to avenge you of any wrongs! You have a lot to gain in loving and will lose your peace, joy, happiness and salvation in hating.

The next time you open your mouth to put someone down, remember when you sow a wind, you will reap a whirlwind (Hosea 8:7a). You will get it back double or more! Let us love one another!

When the spirit of God resides in you, you can love unconditionally and don't expect any love in return! God loves us all! Dear friends, let us love one another, for love comes from God. Everyone who loves has been born of God and knows God. God knows them that are His.

We know and believe the love that God has to us. God is love, and he that dwells in love dwells in God and God in him (1 John 4:16).

CHALLENGE
Accountability

The Lord said this is a wake-up call to the Saints! You are accountable for showing love! 1 John 4:7-8 says, "Beloved, let us love one another, for love is from God, and whoever loves has been born of God and knows God. Anyone who does not love does not know God, because God is love (1 John 4:8)." You are commanded to love!

When someone you know or God forbid a family member is sick unto death, oh how you show love to them! There is nothing you can't do for them! Before they call to ask you, you are there! Wow! If they need anything within your power to do it, you are there! So much love all of a sudden! The Word says in John 13:34-35 (ESV) "A new commandment I give to you, that you love one another: just as I have loved you, you also are to love one another. By this all people will know that you are my disciples, if you have love for one another."

You are not of God if you don't love others. Don't wait too wait to show love! Make time to let people you know that you love them.

Before they were sick unto death, where was your love Saints? Where was your caring? Where were your even monthly visits to check up on them? Our love as Saints is slack! Jesus said to love one another! Love is an action word! You can say you love someone, and they feel that you love them, but until you show your love it's just love talk! Wake up Saints! You are sleeping on the job and some don't even think something is wrong with it! The church seems to have become insensitive to the caring and needs of others. Members lose loved ones, and no one seems to care. I mean really care. To care means to show love not talk love. You are accountable for your actions.

Love talk makes you feel good! Love talk makes you feel justified! Love talk even to others about how you love makes you feel so full! Love talk is very fulfilling to a person that only shows love when something is wrong! Love talk while the person is sick unto death is sometimes just to see how much you can get out of them when they die! Love talk makes you feel so good inside! Love talk is very selfish and un-Christian! That's why you hear about people dying and no one even knew they were sick! They would rather die alone than to have a bunch of phonies around them when they are sick unto death! Wake Up Saints!

Wake up Saints! Some don't even bother to show love at all! Well, how can you say you love God (praising and worshipping the God of Love) whom you have not seen and don't show love to those you know!

We are accountable for every idle word! Saints, surely when Jesus said when you did it to the least of them, you did it unto Him! He was telling us the importance of love! Jesus loved and died for us! What an example! Wake up Saints!

Its Accountability and Responsibility Time! Forgive, Let Go and Let God show you how to love unconditional! You can have the gift of prophecy and understand all mysteries and faith to remove mountains and have not love then you are nothing. You can bestow all your goods to feed the poor and give your body to be burned and have not love then it profits you nothing. Love rejoices not in iniquity but rejoices in the truth.

Love suffers long, is kind, envies not, boasts not of itself and not puffed up. Love does not behave itself unseemly, seeks not its own, is not easily provoked and thinks no evil. Love conquers a multitude of sin. Love bears all things; hopes for all things; endures all things. Love never fails. Prophecies fail, tongues cease, and knowledge vanishes away but love endures (1 Corinthians 13:2-8).

For God so loved us that He gave His only begotten son to give His life for us that were undeserving! Shouldn't our lives reflect the love given to us to others that are undeserving! Love others the way you want to be loved! Treat others the same way you want to be treated. Love not because of but in spite of! Wake Up Saints!

If you forgive others, God will forgive you (Matthew 6:14). Our Lord is good and ready to forgive us and plenteous in mercy unto all of us that call upon Him (Psalm 86:5).

We have redemption through His blood, the forgiveness of sins, according to the riches of His grace (Ephesians 1:7).

Let us love in action not in words only! Love is what it does not what it says only! Be changed! Be Loving! Be who God called you to be not what circumstances, situations or people say or cause you to be!

CHALLENGE
God Allows It

Since nothing happens to us unless God allows it then everything, every problem and situation has a divine appointed time and appointed length of time! God allows things to happen for our spiritual growth. All things work together for good to them that love God and to them who are the called according to His purpose (Romans 8:28). We are called according to His purpose! His purpose is greater than anything that you may encounter in this life. His purpose for you is greater than any sickness, bullying, depression, disease, problem, situation, circumstances or people. Trust God with His purpose for your life!

The Words instructs us to glory in tribulations, knowing that tribulation works toward our patience; and patience, experience; and experience, hope. (Romans 5:34). God, Himself comforts us in all our tribulation (2 Corinthians 1:3-4). Suffering produces endurance/perseverance and perseverance, character and character hope (Romans 5:3-4 NIV).

There is a reason for everything that God allows you to go through! He knows the reason and if you believe and trust Him, He will bring your through! If He brings you to it, He will bring you through it! His purpose for you will be fulfilled. Every one that is called by His name, He created for His glory, formed him and made him (Isaiah 43:7). For the Lord of hosts has purposed and who shall disannul it? And His hand is stretched out, and who shall turn it back? There is nothing or no one that can stop God's purpose for your life from being fulfilled. Work your purpose!

After we have suffered a while, Christ Jesus, will make us perfect, stablish, strengthen and settle us (1 Peter 5:10). The righteous will go through many afflictions, but the Lord delivers us out of them all (Psalm 34:19). For our light affliction, which is but for a moment, works for us a far more exceeding and eternal weight of glory (2 Corinthians 4:17).

God has thoughts that He thinks of you of peace, and not evil, to give you an expected end (Jeremiah 29:11). He already knows your end. You have to just trust Him with all your heart, lean not unto your own understanding, but in all your ways acknowledge Him, and He shall direct your paths (Proverbs 3:5-6). God has sworn saying, surely, He hath thought, so shall it come to pass; and as He has purposed, so shall it stand (Isaiah 14:24). God is in control. We have been predestinated according to God's purpose after the counsel of His own will (Ephesians 1:11).

If God brings you to it, He will bring you through it. God is in control of everything! In this life, we will have to go through some things due to the example that Christ left for us to follow in His steps. Christ suffered for us. (1 Corinthians 13:3) so we will go through many things. Don't worry or fret! We are more than conquerors through Christ that loved us (Romans 8:37).

Our God Rules in the kingdom of men (Daniel 4:7)! God is our refuge and strength, a very ever-present help in trouble (Psalm 46:1). God Will Come Through Every Time!

CHALLENGE
Key to the Kingdom: WEAPONS

We must use the authority that God gave us! God gave us the keys to the kingdom of heaven. Matthew 16:19 says, And I will give unto thee the keys of the kingdom of heaven: and whatsoever thou shalt bind on earth shall be bound in heaven: and whatsoever thou shalt loose on earth shall be loosed in heaven). Your power is no good if you do not use it! Use your keys to bind sickness, diseases, evil spirits, etc. God gave you the keys but it's up to you to live so you can use them.

Do you ever wonder why the enemy just keeps using the same old thing all the time! Wonder why you just can't seem to get over some things!! Its spiritual warfare! We have to bind and rebuke these spirits in the name of Jesus that attack us!

Behold, I give unto you power to tread on serpents and scorpions, and over all the power of the enemy: and nothing shall by any means hurt you (Luke 10:19). If you don't live a righteous life, you can't use the power that God has given unto you. The effectual fervent prayers of the righteous avail much. Righteous prayers reach heaven. God's ears are open to the prayers of the righteous. Wake up saints! The power God gave you is no good if you can't access it.

You must live a righteous and holy life before God to access your power to tread on serpents and scorpions, and over all the power of the enemy so that nothing shall be any means hurt you. Let go of anything that has you stagnated or bound. Let go and be equipped with the power God has given to the righteous. Live So You Can Get Your Keys to Access Your Power!

Be not overcome of evil but overcome evil with good (Romans 12:21). Use your weapon to defeat evil. Treat people the way you want to be treated even if you are treated wrong by them. Vengeance belongs to God anyways. Overcome Evil with Good!

WEAPON: ARMOUR

We argue, fuss and fight among ourselves and it's not even flesh and blood, its spiritual wickedness in high places. For we wrestle not against flesh and blood, but against principalities, against powers, against the rulers of the darkness of this world, against spiritual wickedness in high places (Ephesians 6:12). Know your enemy! For the weapons of our warfare are not carnal, but mighty through God to the pulling down of strong holds; (2 Corinthians 10:4). We have mighty weapons of warfare!

Put on the whole armour of God, that ye may be able to stand against the wiles (devil schemes) of the devil. For we wrestle (our struggle) not against flesh and blood, but against principalities, against powers, against the rulers the darkness of this world, against spiritual wickedness in high places.

Wherefore take unto you the whole armour of God, that ye may be able to withstand (stand your ground NIV) in the evil day, and having done all, to stand.

Stand (firm NIV) therefore, having your loins girt (*Girding the loins* means to be prepared for readiness, strength or endurance in every way possible to follow Christ (belt of truth buckled around your waist NIV), and having on the breastplate of righteousness (means to obey God's commandments and live in a way that is honorable to Him. Psalm 106:3 says, "How blessed are those who keep justice, who practice righteousness at all times!); And your feet shod (fitted) with the preparation (readiness NIV) of the gospel of peace (the good news of Christ brings peace); Put On the Whole Armour of God And Keep It On 24/7!!

Above all, taking the shield of faith, wherewith ye shall be able to quench all the fiery darts of the wicked (quench/end all the flaming arrows of the evil one).

And take the helmet of salvation (hope of salvation), and the sword of the Spirit, which is the word of God:

Praying always with all prayer and supplication in the Spirit, and watching (be alert NIV) thereunto with all perseverance and supplication for all saints; And this is the confidence that we have in Him, that, if we ask any thing according to His will, He heareth us: And if we know that He hear us, whatsoever we ask, we know that we have the petitions that we desired of Him (1 John 5:14:15)

The Word of God gives us more weapons to use and we need all the weapons for our warfare. Our spiritual weapons are mighty through God, in His strength—not ours. We must learn to connect to the strength of the Holy Spirit which

enables us to be victorious in our lives!

WEAPON: FORGIVENESS

For if ye forgive men their trespasses, your heavenly Father will also forgive you:

But if ye forgive not men their trespasses, neither will your Father forgive your trespasses (Matthew 6:14-15). You must forgive! Forgive so you can be set free. Stop spiritual stagnation by forgiving others of the things said or done to you. Don't be bound anymore/ Refuse to be bound by your past which hinders your future growth.

Forgive to live beyond the past that is behind you! Forgive to live to the fulness Christ has planned for you! Don't be stagnated anymore!

To whom ye forgive anything, I forgive also: for if I forgave anything, to whom I forgave it, for your sakes forgave I it in the person of Christ; Lest Satan should get an advantage of us: for we are not ignorant of his devices (2 Corinthians 10-11). If you forgive others, then Christ forgives you. Let it go! Set yourself free! Set your family free! Satan wants to keep you bound by unforgiveness so you will never reach or achieve the greatness that God has for you.

Take the limit off you by using your weapon of forgiveness. Forgive and be set free! Forgive and live life to the fulness no longer bound to a hurtful past. Let go and Let God set you free!

WEAPON: LOVE

And above all things have fervent charity among yourselves: for charity shall cover the multitude of sins (1 Peter 4:8). True charity, Christian love, flows from that holiest love. "Love is of God, and every one that loves is born of God, and knoweth God." God is love! Love is Powerful! Be kindly affectioned one to another with brotherly love; in honour preferring one another (Romans 12:10). Love is not selfish. For God loved us that He gave. And we have known and believed the love that God hath to us.

God is love; and he that dwelleth in love dwelleth in God, and God in him (1 John 4:16). If you love God, then you will love everybody and that includes your enemies which you are commanded to love. Love is a powerful weapon. Love is so powerful.

When you love like Jesus, you just keep on forgiving and loving the ones that did you wrong. Jesus teaches us to keep forgiving over and over again. Love! Love! Love one another! Never tire of loving so never tire of forgiving. Let it go and grow spiritual. Don't be stagnated any more by holding onto things done to you. Our God is bigger than anything He allows us to go through. Believe and trust Him to give you peace in the midst of it all.

Love the Lord thy God with all thy heart, and with all thy soul, and with all thy mind, and with all thy strength: this is the first commandment (Mark 12:30-31). You are commanded to love!

WEAPON: THE WORD OF GOD:

"... and the sword of the Spirit, which is the word of God" (Ephesians 6:17). We defeat Satan by using the weapons of our warfare that are mighty through God. One of the most powerful weapons is the Word of God. For the word of God is quick, and powerful, and sharper than any two-edged sword, piercing even to the dividing asunder of soul and spirit, and of the joints and marrow, and is a discerner of the thoughts and intents of the heart (Hebrews 4:12). NOW THAT'S POWER!

You can't access the power unless you read and study the word. You must make time to read the Word. The Word is what saved us and what will keep us saved. If you hide God's word in your heart, you might not sin against Him. Read the Word and grow spiritually. The Word of God will set you free!

The Word of God will give you power to forgive! The Word of God will strengthen you and sustain you in the midst of trials so you can come out victorious! The Word of God heals, delivers, break chains, sets the captive free and breaks strongholds, etc.! Access the Word of God to Stop Spiritual Stagnation TODAY!

Observe and hear all these words which I command thee, that it may go well with thee, and with thy children after thee forever, when thou doest that which is good and right in the sight of the LORD thy God (Deuteronomy 12:28). Observe and hear the Word of God!

The Word provides a covenant for us if we do that which is good and right in the sight of God. Live a life that is pleasing to God to access the Power of His Word!

Jesus was led up of the Spirit into the wilderness to be tempted of the devil. And when He had fasted forty days and forty nights, He was afterward a hungered. And when the tempter came to Him, he said, If thou be the Son of God, command that these stones be made bread.

But he answered and said, It is written, Man shall not live by bread alone, but by every word that proceedeth out of the mouth of God (Matthew 4:1-4). If Jesus had to use the Word when tempted by Satan, what about you? Keep a word in your heart! Keep a Word on your mind, soul and spirit.

WEAPON: NAME OF JESUS:

Therefore God highly exalted Him and gave Him the name which is above every name, that at the name of Jesus every knee should bow, of those in heaven and on earth and under the earth, and every tongue should confess that Jesus Christ is Lord, to the glory of God the Father (Philippians 2:9-11). The name of Jesus is Powerful!

For where two or three are gathered together IN MY NAME, there am I in the midst of them (Matthew 18:20)." God is in the midst when two or three are gathered together in the name of Jesus. There is power when coming together in the name of Jesus. There is power in the name of Jesus to deliver you from whatever has you bound.

There is power in the name of Jesus to unlock any door that God wants you to walk through. To access your power, you must be set free from whatever have you bound. You must forgive others and let go of whatever has you stagnated. You are the only one standing in your way to fulfil your destiny. And these signs shall follow them that believe; IN MY NAME shall they cast out devils; they shall speak with new tongues (Mark 16:17.;" Praise God! In the name of Jesus, you can cast out devils. In order to be able to access this weapon, you must have a prayer life and fast for "this kinds".

Jesus teaches us that we must fast and pray to be able to have the power and authority to be victorious when confronted or called upon to pray in the name of Jesus to get a prayer through. You can't be stagnated or bound when in warfare. You must stay prayerful and fast often. In the name of Jesus, you have the victory!

And whatsoever ye shall ask IN MY NAME, that will I do, that the Father may be glorified in the Son. If ye shall ask any thing IN MY NAME, I will do it (John 14:13-14). God has given us power and authority in His name! You must live a holy and righteous life so you can access this power and use it!

"Ye have not chosen me, but I have chosen you, and ordained you, that ye should go and bring forth fruit, and that your fruit should remain: that whatsoever ye shall ask of the Father IN MY NAME, he may give it you (John 15:16).

And in that day ye shall ask me nothing. Verily, verily, I say unto you, Whatsoever ye shall ask the Father IN MY NAME, he will give it you. Hitherto have ye asked nothing IN MY NAME: ask, and ye shall receive, that your joy may be full. These things have I spoken unto you in proverbs: but the time cometh, when I shall no more speak unto you in proverbs, but I shall shew you plainly of the Father. At that day ye shall ask IN MY NAME: and I say not unto you, that I will pray the Father for you (John 16:23–26):

Jesus promises to pray to the Father for us! What a covering! Our Savior is watching out for us! No good thing would He withhold from us! Get Connected! Stay Connected!

If you feel disconnected from the power that's supposed to work within you, call on the name of Jesus! He answers you before you call. Call Him Jesus! Jesus! Jesus! Jesus said, And, behold, I send the promise of my Father upon you: but tarry ye…, until ye be endued with power from on high (Luke 24:49).

Call Him while He may be found. Call Him! Seek Him! He promised to answer. Call Him to set you free! Call Him to heal and deliver you from sicknesses, diseases, situations, problems and circumstances beyond your control. You don't have to be stagnated any longer. In the name of Jesus, you are more than a conqueror! In the name of Jesus, you have

the victory.

WEAPON: TESTIMONY:

They overcame him by the blood of the Lamb and by the word of their testimony, and they loved not their lives unto the death (Revelation 12:11).

Don't allow the enemy to deceive you! If you use your testimony of what God did for you before of healing, deliverance; restoring your peace, joy and happiness; working out problems and situations; and meeting your needs; you will stand victoriously in faith that God will come through for you again and again in everything that concerns you! He did it before! He can do it again! You Can Stand on His Spoken Word! His Word Shall Stand Throughout IT ALL!

Ye are of God, little children, and have overcome them: because greater is He that is in you, than he that is in the world (1 John 4:4). The God in you is greater than anything in this world. Hold unto God's unchanging hands. The God in you will give you the victory in all things. The God in you will help you overcome any obstacles or problems that you may encounter.

When confronted with situations, problems, sickness or diseases, know that the God in you is greater than that. The God in you is greater than anything or anyone that you may encounter. The God in you is greater than those that talked about you, put you down, stole from you, mistreated you, lied on you, despitefully used you, bullied you and drove you to the point of thinking of suicide. He's greater! He's greater than it all!

Let go and let God deliver you. You can truly testify that God is good all the time!

For whatsoever is born of God overcometh the world: and this is the victory that overcometh the world, even our faith (1 John 5:4). Being born of God is a spiritual birth of the Holy Spirit. When we are born of God, we have a new heart. When you turn your life over to God, He will make you an overcomer. Being born again, your life reflects who you serve. Being born of God, you become transformed by the renewing of your mind. It's a spiritual birth. You become changed. You are an overcomer.

The God in you is greater than anything in this world. You are an overcomer. Your faith is a testimony to what God is doing, has done and will do for you. Who is he that overcometh the world, but he that believeth that Jesus is the Son of God? (1 John 5:5). Believe and be set free! Be an overcomer and not be stagnated anymore! Be free! Stay free!

WEAPON: THANKSGIVING

Be anxious for nothing, but in everything, by prayer and supplication with gratitude, make your requests known to God. And the peace of God, which surpasses all understanding, will protect your hearts and minds through Christ Jesus (Philippians 4:6-7).

The enemy wants you to be depressed, distraught, discontented, feel deserted, have anxiety, worry, envy, covetousness, gossip, complaining and have slander in your heart. Through thankfulness, God is able to adjust your heart so your prayers will no longer be selfish prayers but prayers He can answer. You are to pray according to His divine will, way, plan and purpose for your life!

In everything give thanks: for this is the will of God in Christ Jesus concerning you (1 Thessalonians 5:18). Give thanks to God for everything. Thank God for the good and the bad because even the bad got to work together for your good. It may not feel good but thank God.

The God in you is greater than any trial or tribulation that He allows you to go through. If He brings you to it, He will bring you through it.

Just thank God for the victory even before you see the victory. Just thank Him for healing, deliverance, being set free, victory and overcoming even before it has come into fruition. It shall come to pass! A Change is going to come!

By him therefore let us offer the sacrifice of praise to God continually, that is, the fruit of our lips giving thanks to his name (Hebrews 13:15). It's a sacrifice of praise when you don't see God moving but thank and praise Him for the victory that shall come to pass.

It's a sacrifice of praise when you don't see your way or you're going through a lack, depression or even stagnated. Thank God for bringing you out before you come out. Thank God for deliverance while you still bound. Thank God for making a way even before He has made a way.

Just keep thanking and praising God because you know He is able to deliver you from anything. Thank Him for setting you free even when you still feel bound. You are more than a conqueror through Christ Jesus.

WEAPON: THE POWER OF YOUR PRAISE

Praise God with your whole heart and sing praises unto Him. Worship and praise Him for His lovingkindness and for His truth: His name is to be praised and magnified. When you cry, He will answer you and strengthen you with strength in your soul (Psalm 138:1-3).

I will praise thee with my whole heart: before the gods will I sing praise unto thee. I will worship toward thy holy temple and praise thy name for thy lovingkindness and for thy truth: for thou hast magnified thy word above all thy name. In the day when I cried, thou answeredst me, and strengthenedst me with strength in my soul (Psalm138:1-3).

I will bless the LORD at all times: His praise shall continually be in my mouth. Keep a praise on your mind! Bless the Lord at all times. Thank Him continually for His grace and mercy that endures forever. I sought the LORD, and He heard me, and delivered me from all my fears (Psalm 34:1, 4). If you seek God, He will hear you and deliver you!

The Lord's eyes are upon the righteous, and His ears are open to your cry (Psalm 34:15). O give thanks unto the LORD; for he is good; for his mercy endureth forever. (1 Chronicles 16:34). His eyes are always looking upon you if you are righteous. In order to have God's eyes always beholding you, you must live a holy and righteous life.

You must forgive anyone that hurt you in the present or in the past. In order to reach God, you cannot be bound and stagnated! If you don't forgive others neither will He forgive you! Let go and Let God deliver you! Be set free!

And when they began to sing and to praise, the LORD set ambushments against... (the enemy) (2 Chronicles 20:22a).

The LORDs shall fight for you, and ye shall hold your peace (John 14:14). God stepped into the fight when they began to sing and to praise the Lord. There is power in singing and praising God! When you hold your peace or be still, God will fight your battles.

Praise God like it's already done! Praise Him like you're already healed and delivered! Praise Him like your needs have already been met! Praise Him like the victory is yours already! Praise Him like you have already overcome every obstacle, problem, situation, circumstances, sickness or diseases! Praise Him because you're an overcomer!

The battle is the Lord's and the victory is yours! God inhabits your praises (Psalm 22:3)! When you continue to praise God, He inhabits or dwells with you! Praising God ushering in His presence. He will come! He will come and be with you! When going through trials and tribulations, be of good cheer, Blessed be God, even the Father of our Lord Jesus Christ, the Father of mercies, and the God of all comfort; Who comforteth us in all our tribulation, that we may be able to comfort them which are in any trouble, by the comfort wherewith we ourselves are comforted of God (2 Corinthians 1:3-4). You don't need to worry or fret because God will comfort you.

During the times of suffering, God gives us comfort and encouragement through His Word (2 Corinthians 1:3-4). Praise your way through any trials and tribulations that come your way! God is with you. When God is for you, who can be against you? He's more than the whole world against you.

For of him, and through him, and to him, are all things: to whom be glory forever (Romans 11:36). Amen. All the glory, honor and praise belongs to God for its through Him that we live and move. He's our creator! Be grateful! Be thankful!

The very moment that you began to stop worrying and fretting and start shouting and praising the LORD, the Lord will set a surprise attack against anything that's troubling you. Your Praise will confuse the enemy. The enemy wants to keep you depressed, distressed, disappointed, distracted, distraught, and many other things.

Use your Weapon of Praise! Just start singing and praising God and watch God move on your behalf and defeat the enemy. Just began singing and praising God and watch Him confuse and defeat whatever tries to come up against you. All things work together for good to them that love God, to them who are the called according to His purpose (Romans 8:28). It's all going to work out for your good! All of it!

Without faith it is impossible to please Him: for he that cometh to God must believe that He is, and that He is a rewarder of them that diligently seek Him (Hebrews 11:6). You must believe that God is first, and that He will reward you if you earnestly seek Him by reading His word and praying to Him.

There is no limit to the miracles and blessings you can obtain through the power of praise! Praise is what we do when we want to get closer to God! Praise unlocks the door of your heart to rejoice no matter what it seems like, looks like or appears to be!

You can praise your way through anything! Bound, wounded, chained - just start praising God and feel the uplifting as God comes! God inhabits your praises (Psalm 22:3)! Praise God until you get your breakthrough in Jesus name! Praise God until you feel His presence for in His presence is fullness of joy!

When Praises go up blessings, healing, miracles, breakthroughs, deliverance, shackles loosed, strongholds are broken, chains broken, peace, love, joy and happiness will come down! Praise Him like its already done! Praise

Him for you are fearfully and wonderfully made: marvelous are His works; and that your soul knows that (Psalm 139:14). He hath made all things beautiful in His time (Ecclesiastes 3:11a). Praise Him!

Bless the LORD with your whole soul. Bless His holy name, Bless the Lord and forget not all His benefits. He forgives all your iniquities and who heals all your diseases (Psalm 103:1-3). Bless the Lord means to express our wholehearted gratitude and delight to Him for all that He does for us! Praise your way through!

'Same God! Same Resurrection Power! Same Healing and Deliverance Power! Same God, Same Power Operating Right Now! REMEMBER: YOU CAN PRAISE YOUR WAY THROUGH ANYTHING.

CHALLENGE
Delayed Promises

Delayed promises of God always have a purpose! No matter what it looks like, seems like or appears to be, God will keep His Word.

God will perform that which He hath spoken into your life! Don't allow delays, denials and the ever-increasing presence of evil shake your faith. Never waver in believing God's promise. For the LORD of hosts hath purposed, and who shall disannul it? and his hand is stretched out, and who shall turn it back? (Isaiah 14:27). What God has spoken; He will do.

God will do just what He said. Nothing or no one can stop God's blessings from being manifested in your life. When God's hands are stretched out to bless you, nothing or no one can curse what God called blessed. It shall come to pass.

Be patient and wait on the Lord. There is a blessing in hoping, trusting and waiting on the Lord. They that wait upon the LORD shall renew their strength; they shall mount up with wings as eagles; they shall run, and not be weary; and they shall walk, and not faint (Isaiah 40:31). If you wait on the Lord, your strength shall be renewed. You will not get weary in well doing because the Lord fights your battles.

It doesn't matter what's going on in your life, God has thoughts of peace and not evil toward you. He also has thoughts of an expected end for your life (Jeremiah 29:11). No matter what it looks like, appears to be or if the promises seem to be delayed, He shall come through every time. Wait on the Lord and encouraged. God will perfect everything that concerns you. He may not come when you want Him, but He always comes on time. Just remember:

There is nothing too hard for the Lord. There is no problem that He can't solve. There is no situation that He can't work out. There is no sickness that He can't heal and deliver.

The eyes of the Lord are in every place, beholding the evil and the good (Proverbs 15:3). It doesn't matter where you go, He sees you. There is nothing in creation hidden from God's sight. Just trust Him with all your heart, lean not unto your own understanding; in all your ways acknowledge Him and He shall direct your paths (Proverbs 3:5-6).

God's purpose for your life was established even before you were born. He chose you before the foundation of the world, that you should be holy and without blame before Him in love (Ephesians 1:4). The foundation of God stands sure, having a seal, the Lord knows them that are His (2 Timothy 2:19).

God knows who you are. You must have a personal relationship with Him. You must have faith in Him. You must believe! You must believe that He is, and that He is a rewarder of them that diligently seek Him (Hebrews 11:6).

God has promised that He will never leave us nor forsake us and that all things will work for our good! Believe God's Word and His promises! There is no failure in God. God won't fail you! The word that God speaks shall not return unto Him void, but it shall accomplish that which He please and it shall prosper in the He sends it to do (Isaiah 55:11). If your promises are delayed, know that God's word will stand, and He shall come through. Delayed does not mean denied!

IN CONCLUSION

This book is to encourage you to stand fast in your faith and never waver. When you waver, your blessings flow away from you. You must believe to receive anything from God. There will always be obstacles, problems, situations, sicknesses, diseases and weapons that will form but shall not prosper.

There is nothing that God can't deliver you out of or from! When you are in God's hands even the devil in hell cannot take you out. There is a place in God where the devil can't do you any harm. He that dwells in the secret place of the Most High shall abide under the shadow of the Almighty (Psalm 91:1). You must submit yourselves to God. Resist the devil and he will flee from you.

Stand fast therefore in the liberty wherewith Christ hath made us free and be not entangled again with the yoke of bondage (Galatians 5:1). Don't allow anyone or anything to bind you again. Once Christ has made you free, stay free! Be loosed and not bound again! Be loosed from anyone or anything that had you bound or stagnated. Be loosed from anything that causes you to disconnect from Christ.

Now the Lord is that Spirit: and where the Spirit of the Lord is, there is liberty (2 Corinthians 3:17). Stay connected to the Spirit of the Lord so you can be loosed from whatever may have you bound. If the Son shall make you free, you shall be free indeed (James 8:36). Stay connected to The Source of your power for healing and deliverance. For by Jesus' stripes, you are healed. God didn't bring you this far for you to be bound again. Get Free! Stay Free! Live Free! Stay Free! Stay Loosed! Be Forever Changed!

The same God that stopped the Red Sea from flowing can stop or block anything that tries to cause you any evil, hurt, harm or danger. You must be equipped. Put on the whole armor of God. Don't be stagnated! Grow in God's grace and mercy toward you! Be Forever Changed in Jesus name!

Made in the USA
Columbia, SC
10 July 2020

13657320R00098